This book was b

Hustle University (Hustle U) is an institution of higher learning for today's Independent Minded Entrepreneur.

The mission of **Hustle University** is to promote entrepreneurialism and leadership through personal development, empowerment and the teachings of proven success strategies.

www.HustleUniversity.Org

THE HUSTLER'S 10 COMMANDMENTS

A Collection of Corporate Best Practices, Ancient Wisdom and Guerilla Tactics for Today's Independent Minded Entrepreneur

THE HUSTLER'S 10 COMMANDMENTS

*A Collection of Corporate Best Practices,
Ancient Wisdom and Guerilla Tactics for
Today's Independent Minded Entrepreneur*

By Hotep

SKINNYMEN PRODUCTIONS
New York   Atlanta   Los Angeles

The Hustler's 10 Commandments

www.hustlers10commandments.com

ISBN #978-0-9800232-0-6

Published by: Skinnymen Productions, Stone Mountain, GA 30083

Skinnymen Productions, its logos and marks are trademarks of Skinnymen Productions.

Manufactured in the United States of America

Printed by Selfpublishing.com

Second Printing, May 2007

Photography by OPP Studios

PUBLISHER'S NOTE: This work is a labor of love. It is the result of my attending the **School of Hard Knocks** where I received a B.A. in *Failed Ideas*, a Masters Degree in *Bad Investments*, and a PhD in *Poor Time Management*. Names, characters, places, and incidents are either the product of the author's experiences or are used with permission, and any resemblance to actual persons, living or dead, business establishments, events, or locales is entirely on purpose.

To my parents, Felicia A. Scotland AND Ramon A. Benzo (RIP), Thank you for naming me after great people and making sure I grow into the crown that you placed soaring above my head. It is only by standing on your shoulders that I am able to reach so high!

To my Wife, You are the apple of my eye; the Sun in my sky. Everybody knows I love my Babykakes!

To my heroes, Marcus Garvey, Malcolm X, and Muhammad Ali.

I also dedicate this book to everyone whose life has inspired me, and to everyone that this book will touch. Manifest your Destiny!

Aight!

Peace!

ACKNOWLEDGEMENTS:

Mom- who continues to encourage me to do more, become better and greater**, Pops**- for providing me with the studies of ancient African Culture and Eastern theology and philosophy, **My Wife** for keeping me balanced and grounded, **Grandma Kenni & Grandma Benzo**- for being the roots of our family trees. **Dr. Coleman** for spiritual guidance, **Big Tah** (my brother from another mother) for dropping the seed of the idea for me to write an actual book, **Fort Knox** for being a "nice nigga" (you're still the livest brother I know), **Nancy Gilliam** and **Denise Spiller** of AALM for holding the best conference I'd ever attended (it is because of your event that I decided to write this book!), **Wess** (fellow Garveyite)- you are the TRUE documentarian! Thank you for rollin' with me. **Leslie Greene**- for believing in my documentary's vision b4 it was manifested, **Kim Wilson**- for jump-starting my filmmaking career. **Troya Sampson** for being the first person to REALLY get behind my vision and *cheerlead* for Hotep & Skinnymen Productions (you're forever my ace!), **Leticia** (Docugraphix)- for being my first major sponsor. **Mimi Cartier** – for continually being such a blessing and so thoughtful, **Kehinde Thompson**- the hottest photographer I know (it's your turn)! **KeyC-** for years of tech support and reliability. **Nadra**- one of the few truly GOOD BROTHERS I know, **Caustic Mimi**- (*"Goin' to the Grammys"*) you're my sister-in-arms and I got your back! **Rosalind**- the epitome of Hottentot Venus- you were MY counselor! **Bro Malik**- the other good brother I know. To all the contributing writers- your life lessons are priceless! Thank you for sharing them. To those I missed…..my humble apologies. I love you all!

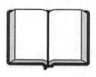

TABLE OF CONTENTS

THE MEANING OF THE NAME:

Born in Queens, NYC in the early 1970's, I represent the generation of people born at the exact moment the culture of Hip-Hop emerged from the womb of urban America.

The oldest of 3 boys, I always considered Hip-Hop to be my adopted BIG BROTHER. We grew up together. He taught me much of what I know and understand today. He taught me how to breakdance, showed me how to rock my gear (be fashionable), instructed me on the fine art of graffiti, helped me win the hearts of many women, challenged me to think critically, taught me lessons in Black History and showed me different parts of the country. But, most importantly, my big brother Hip-Hop gave me a positive self-image, a sense of self-worth and belonging.

Hip-Hop carried me under his wing until I graduated high school. It was during my freshman year at college that I first stepped from under his shadow, and started to define my own path. I started to set my own trends in hair, fashion, dance and music instead of copying the ones Hip-Hop created. **It was like one of those moments in Kung-Fu movies when the student had learned so well, he was able to match or defeat his Master.** My brother Hip-Hop had helped raise me to a point where I understood that I AFFECT AND INFLUENCE THE CULTURE AS MUCH AS IT DOES ME.

This leads me to explain the reason for the title, "**The Hustler's 10 Commandments**".

A current trend in today's Hip-Hop is the overuse (and mis-use) of the term, *hustler*. EVERYBODY claims to be a hustler! The word HUSTLE has 2 meanings; a "standard" definition and a *street* or *slang* definition.

The *Standard* definition: Hustle- verb; to act aggressively especially in business dealings.

The *Street/ Slang* definition: Hustle- verb; 1. to make money covertly, often illegally. 2. To sell drugs. 3. To pursue financial gains by any means necessary. Hustle- noun; a side job. Work one does outside of their 9-5 job.

Hip-Hop identifies mainly with the street definition. This fact was fine with me until multi-million dollar companies **bought the image of Hip-Hop**. Once this was done, the corporations twisted the artform and culture in despicable ways. Illegal hustles were turned into today's careers of choice, and immoral hustler's (criminals) were magically transformed into today's leaders and heroes for our youth. This is a BIG PROBLEM!

In order to balance the scales (being the Libra that I am), I chose to champion for the **standard definition of hustle**.

My mission: to create a hard-hitting manual, filled with empowering lessons, in order to change lives and save the world (and universe) from the evil mind control of greedy corporations, who intend to deceive and enslave the masses by employing weapons of illusion, confusion and destruction. *(whew!)*

The title, **The Hustler's 10 Commandments** allowed me to capitalize off 3 of today's biggest markets: Hip-Hop, Entrepreneurs, and Church- goers. This was a strategic move to maximize my reach. Therefore, more books get sold, more people's lives get touched and more money gets made.

Cuz let's not forget.............I'M A HUSTLER TOO!

- Hotep, (formerly also known as *Hustle Simmons)*

Hotep rocks the classic, old-school sheepskin and "Mr. Hollywood" sunglasses @ his movie premiere.

FOREWORD:

Writing this book was like having my own *"Jerry Maguire"* moment. It's like a manifesto that was whispered (and sometimes shouted) to me by the Creator through my family, peers, mentors and true life experience.

I liken the moments of inspiration for writing this book to the story of Moses, who is credited with receiving the original 10 Commandments directly as God spoke to him.

"God told me to do it!"

- Hotep

THE FIRST COMMANDMENT

YOUR NETWORK IS YOUR NET WORTH.

CHAPT 1: YOUR NETWORK IS YOUR NET WORTH

Net worth is commonly known as the difference between what you *own* and what you *owe*. You can figure your net worth by adding all your debts (credit cards, mortgages, car loans, and/or anything else you owe) and subtracting that sum from your total assets (home value, stocks, cash, furniture, electronics and anything else you own of value).

Net worth is not an actual pile of physical dollars, but more a summation of the *potential dollar amount* that your assets would bear if you liquidated (sold) them. It is with this same summation of **potential** that we can include our network (friends, crew, gang, homies, posse) as assets too.

"Birds of a feather, flock together."

Remember when you were little, and your mother told you to be careful who you choose as friends? Well, that advice doesn't change with age. Your friends will either help bring you up, or take you down. They can be assets, or liabilities.

It was once suggested to me that I make a list of people in my life that I can count **on**, and those I can count **out**. Doing so, (and spending the majority of my time with those that I could count on) drastically improved my business and social life. The same can and will happen for you.

"If you hang around 4 broke people, you're bound to be the 5th".

This saying would still hold true if you replaced the word *broke* with *rich*, *positive*, *smart* or any other adjective you choose. Such is the power of your **network**.

My cousin calls his network his "Circle of Influence". I think this is a very appropriate term because it recognizes the amazing influence those we surround ourselves with have on us. Your business will flourish if you hang around business savvy people. Your life will start to seem so much more beautiful if your friends are positive and optimistic. You will never be homeless, without food, clothes or money if your circle is affluent. That's because your Network is your Net Worth!

LIFE LESSON:

I have always been one who believed in networking, but it wasn't until very recently that I discovered the truth behind the Hustler's Commandment; your network is your net worth.

After having been away from the literary and media industries for a little over fifteen years, I slowly began transitioning myself back into the business. I started seeking opportunities to promote my children's book which I had self-published. With the aid of the Internet, I began tapping into sources and building a network that would assist me in fulfilling my quest.

I discovered there were many people out there who had an interest in what I was doing and sincerely wanted to help. I received invitations to different events and accepted most. During my travels, I continued to meet like-minded individuals, and my network continued to grow.

As a firm believer in the power of giving, I made it my business to do whatever I could to help someone achieve his or her goals and visions. This included not only disseminating information, but also seizing opportunities to make connections between people that could benefit from each other's talents and experiences. The more that I helped others, the more "fuel" I received to keep the fire of my vision and purpose burning.

The recognition of the value, or net worth of my network came during the African American Literary and Media Conference, which was held February 2006 in Reno, Nevada. This was the AALAM Group's first conference, and it was our vision to create an atmosphere where novices and professionals would be able to receive the tools and inspiration needed to navigate their way through the literary and media industries. My partner Denise and I were faced with many challenges and seemingly insurmountable obstacles. There were critical moments where giving up was the option of choice, but we decided to make the sacrifice and do whatever it would take to make the conference happen.

It was a decision that transformed our lives forever. During that weekend, our network was drawn together from all points within the United States. There are no words to describe the power and synergy that was experienced. People's lives were changed. Relationships were solidified. Projects were birthed. Strength to continue was found in our network.

That weekend helped me discover the importance of being surrounded by positive like-minded individuals who understand the power of giving as

well as receiving. No one person can achieve greatness and realize the power of possibility remaining inside of self. Yes, it is true that your sense of self worth is important, but ultimately it is your network that is your net worth!
- Nancy Gilliam

TASKS:

1) Make a list of the people you can *COUNT ON* and those you can *COUNT OUT*.
2) Build your own" circle of influence" from the people you can *count on*.
3) Spend less time with the people you can *count out*.
4) Identify someone that is successful in your field. See if you can intern for them or have them mentor you.
5) Attend conferences, networking socials where people of similar interest or goals will be.
6) Join organizations, websites, e-zines and join Yahoo groups that are made up of people with similar interest or goals as your own.

THE SECOND COMMANDMENT

IMAGE IS EVERYTHING.

CHAPT 2: IMAGE IS EVERYTHING

They say we should never judge a book by its cover, but it's the *cover* that makes us want to open the book in the first place.

What is truth? Truth is NOT a matter of fact. History has shown us all, that *truth* is only an **idea** that is commonly accepted. Yet laws, policy and judgments are often erroneously made based off of these ideas everyday.

At one time, each of these ideas was once "true":

1) The Earth is flat.
2) Christopher Columbus discovered America.
3) Africa has made no significant contribution to the world.
4) Cocaine is good for you and should be used daily.

Get the picture? Truth is only what we **perceive** it to be. This is why *image* is key. Consumers buy products because of their perception of it. People chose mates because of their *perception* of the other person. Citizens choose leaders based on their *perception* of that candidate. Cops treat people according to their *perception* of the individual. Where is truth in this in this equation? The fact of the matter is: **very little of what we do is based on actual truth.**

God is the only truth. As mere mortals, we can only hope that our perception of things is actually *true*. The understanding of this principal can be a very powerful tool. Image is EVERYTHING.

LIFE LESSON:

Image is everything! For a decade now I have been a natural wearing, strong looking, and unapproachable black woman. My natural made me look like a piece of brick. That was good for me in my personal life, meaning, I had control over things. If I didn't want to be bothered by certain folks, my demeanor would let them know. This was also a bad thing because whether I knew it or not, I seemed to look limited to revolutionary type roles, events, and things. How was I to get the world to realize I was far more than the length of my afro? How was I to let the business/entertainment world know, I wasn't going to commit arson on their property? Or that I wouldn't go on national television and advocate "killing whitey"?

In winter 2005, I actually decided to run an experiment. Now, I have a short processed look and my hair is similar to Nia Long's in "The Best Man". I slightly changed my attire to "simply sophisticated" and I wear eye make-up. I took my new look amongst my co-workers in the entertainment field and they lost their minds. People are digging this new look. Wow! I hadn't changed on the inside at all. I am still stern, intelligent, and no non-sense, but it seemed to not be a factor being I didn't look like Teflon in a dress. I am getting more compliments and people aren't intimidated by me.

Overall, the change was healthy and is deeming itself profitable. Since image is everything, I'm not saying "fake it, til you make it"; I'm saying, "If it ain't working, CHANGE IT!
- Queen (Shanikra Hankins)

TASKS:

1) Make sure your website or product exterior look exceptionally good.
2) Dress the part. *The way you DRESS determines the way you will be ADDRESSED.*
3) Speak clearly and with confidence.
4) Create promotional material to support your business (biz cards, flyers, t-shirts)
5) Keep your vehicle looking nice and well maintained. Of course, a luxury vehicle will make you appear to have money. But please don't over extend your finances for a car.
6) *Peep Game!* Pay attention to Flyers, CDs, Books or DVD covers that catch your eye. Take the time to identify WHY you noticed them and implement those aspects into your own designs.

THE THIRD
COMMANDMENT

THE EARLY BIRD GETS THE WORM.

CHAPT 3: THE EARLY BIRD GETS THE WORM

This chapter is personally relevant to me. I have always struggled with being on time. I've been late for everything from dates, to events, to meetings and airplane flights. A friend once joked and said that I will be late to my own funeral. So, dear readers, please know that I write these words for my own benefit as much as I do for yours.

The concept of time must be respected and held almost sacredly. Why? Because it is one of the very few things in life that never repeats itself. Once it's gone, it's gone......... forever! So, until someone invents a way for humans to travel back in time...... **Respect it**!

In order to maximize the opportunities that are opened before us, we must arrive **on time** to receive them. No. Scratch that.... not "*on time*".........we need to be EARLY!

A school principal once told me, "*To be on time, is to be late*". The truth in this statement wasn't actually apparent to me until I began writing this book.

Please follow this scenario:

You are right on time for your meeting with a record label CEO, book publisher, film distributor....whatever. You walk into her office, make your presentation, ask your questions, smile, shake hands and leave the meeting feeling confident that it went well.....and it did!

*However, because you were simply **on time**, you missed the opportunity to check your appearance in the restroom. If you had, you would have noticed that your zipper was open. Because you were simply **on*** *time*, *you also missed hearing the CEO comment on a meeting she had last week. If you had been there to hear her comments, you would have known not to have given her so many compliments (she really hates that). You also missed her secretary's phone conversation. If you were early enough to hear it, you would have known that a new position at the office had opened up. A position you would have loved to apply for.*

Unfortunately for you, the guy that had a meeting with the CEO after yours was an hour EARLY. He heard all of the conversations and was able to check his appearance. He was relaxed, ready to inquire about the job opening and would not comment on the CEO's good looks.

Who do YOU think made the most of their opportunity?

The EARLY BIRD got the worm!

LIFE LESSON:

I remember my freshman year of college at the University of Pittsburgh in August 1987. It was registration day and I was headed to one of the campus buildings to register for my classes that semester. I wasn't early that morning, and there was a long-ass line in front of me to enter the building. But I noticed immediately that everyone was waiting to go inside one door when there four other doors available to enter the building. So my bold-ass walked up past everyone in line and tried one of the other doors, and it opened. I walked right in past the line; and guess what happened after that.......... half of the other line followed me into the door.

So, although I was not early that day, I had the courage to be first, and being first is parallel to being early. They are similar in that you have no company there with you, and so you may feel awkward, inexperienced and afraid of what may happen. It takes courage and confidence to be first, and eagerness and promptness to be early. Well, generally, I'm an early riser, early starter, early arriver as well, which all lends itself to me being one who is brave, bold, and ready enough to start things on my own. In fact, my whole life has been that way. I was always starting things and getting there early to be first.

Anyway, that's exactly what I did in my career as a young writer. In 1991, among Terry McMillan, Bebe Moore Campbell, Walter Mosley, and E. Lynn Harris, I became the first and youngest author to write about contemporary urban streets since Donald Goines and Iceberg Slim. So I was early, I was first, I'll continue to reinvent the game and I'm still eating those juicy worms with more on the way (smile.)
- Omar Tyree

TASKS:

1) **Set your clock 30 minutes ahead of the actual time.**
2) **Arrive at meetings at least 20 minutes early.**
3) **Arrive at events an hour early.**
4) **Call to confirm appointments 2 hours prior to meeting time.**
5) **Don't procrastinate.**
6) **Turn in assignments before their deadline.**

THE FOURTH COMMANDMENT

IT'S LONELY AT THE TOP.

CHAPT 4: IT'S LONELY AT THE TOP

While using the bathroom at a sports bar, I came across a posted article about Allen Iverson. It was in this unlikely place and from this *bad boy* athlete that I learned a great lesson. In the article was a quote from Iverson that went something like....

*"There are a million people that love me, and a **Billion** people that hate me. I think about those that love me, and keep it moving."*

This statement is the perfect acceptance speech for one that understands the next commandment.

It's lonely at the top.

If you look around yourself and notice you have a lot fewer peers than you used to, it may be a sign that you're getting closer to being successful in your field. Don't let your raggedy, good- for-nothing friends make you feel bad cuz you don't call and hang around them any more. That's the old crabs in a barrel routine; **they would rather pull you down, than see you get out!**

Understand this:

The masses of our world's population are followers, not leaders; consumers, not producers; victims, not victors. They watch too much TV, listen to too much radio and believe everything they see and hear. This phenomenon is no accident. In a capitalist democracy it is an absolute necessity!

Think about your Junior High School years:

As youth, we had the tendency to follow the crowd. We often suffered from the effects of peer pressure. Most of us sought to "*fit in*". For the intelligent, well-behaved child, this often meant **acting** ignorant; and doing things that led to trouble, bad health and lower achievement.

Well, the real world of adults isn't much different. But now, the "crowd" that many of us once sought to emulate is broke, troubled by legal issues, riddled with diseases and see little hope for a better future. **Who wants to be a part of that crowd?**

As you become increasingly successful, wealthy and wise; you will find that you have to distance yourself from your homies of the past. Don't let them run that *"You forgot where you came from"* speech.

You remember where you come from, but you **also know where you are going**. So get ready, cuz it's lonely at the top.

LIFE LESSON:

There is a price to pay for being successful, and most people don't want to pay it. That's why there's Lotto and a whole bunch of infomercials on TV late at night that sell you unrealistic ways to achieve "easy" success.

I manage several musical artists. Every time we reach a certain level of success (such as putting an album out, booking a major show or filming a DVD) other artists approach us begging to be managed by our management team. They see the effects, and want them too. So I direct them right to the cause that made the effect happen.

I invite them to join the team, but on a lower level than they expect. For example: I tell them that we only have room for a hype man when I know they want to be the main rapper. Or I tell them that we need a road manager when I know they would like to be a main manager. Am I just being mean and vindictive? No, I'm requesting that they go through the same process that everyone on the team went through to get where we're at. How does one know that they can handle the pressures of being on the top unless they've been through trials and tribulations?

When you climb to the top, you're forming muscles, courage and wherewithal that will aid you in staying at the top. That's why it's so lonely up there; because most people aren't strong enough to climb the mountain of success. It IS lonely at the top, and I'd rather be alone with my hard working self, than with a group of lazy tag-a-longs. The top of the pyramid is pointed for a reason.
- Big Tah

LIFE LESSON:

*Often times, you hear people say that it is lonely at the top, but what you don't hear people elaborate on is that it is just as lonely **getting** to the top. I am not at the peak of my career yet; however, I still experience loneliness in my quest to reach this point. As an Entertainment Attorney, I have encountered everything from men who reject me due to my earning potential to people being intimidated by my career to people asking me to compromise myself in order to get ahead. I have*

41

heard successful women speak of this before, but there is nothing like experiencing it for yourself. Despite these obstacles and barriers, I continue on the journey even when it means doing so alone.

I have had to leave certain things and people behind in order to accomplish my goals. This has often left me alone to conquer unfamiliar territory, but that is a sacrifice that I willingly make to maximize my potential. Even some of my loved ones do not fully understand the path that I am on. At the end of day, I realize that trailblazers venture into unfamiliar places to make their mark even when it requires the dreadful loneliness that most people fear. It is lonely at the top; and also during the journey to the top as well, but sometimes it is the journey that makes the destination worth it all!
- Keisha R. Perry, Esq.

TASKS:

1) **Make your haters, your MOTIVATORS!**
2) **Seek QUALITY in relationships, not quantity.**
3) **Find peace and happiness in solitude.**
4) **Find a support group of like-minded individuals.**
5) **In times of loneliness, seek companionship in your work.**
6) **Love yourself enough to be happy BY yourself.**

THE FIFTH COMMANDMENT

SUCCESS- WHERE OPPORTUNITY MEETS PREPARATION.

CHAPT 5: SUCCESS- WHERE OPPORTUNITY MEETS PREPARATION

"Tomorrow belongs to the people who prepare for it today". – Malcolm X

Everybody wants to be successful. The question is: *Are you ready for opportunity when it finally knocks*? Will you answer the door with your briefcase, laptop, cell phone and palm pilot ready to roll? Or will you be caught in your pajamas, yawning with cold in your eyes?

"To be prepared is EVERYTHING." (as told to me by my pops)

Let's look at the entertainment/ media industries. Many people in these industries are in pursuit of receiving that ever elusive, life changing "deal". (Record deal, label deal, distribution deal, publishing deal, modeling deal...etc.) Most artists spend countless hours perfecting their craft, but **few** take the necessary steps to fully prepare themselves for the very opportunity that they seek. They may be talented, but most people in the entertainment/ media industries are undoubtedly NOT READY FOR THE BUSINESS OF "THE DEAL".

All too often, the opportunity passes them by, OR they get offered a "deal" that is certainly not in their favor. Either way, **many fail to be successful, because they are simply not prepared.**

LIFE LESSON:

Recently I have been associated with several California companies that strive to create Urban based distribution deals for audio & video projects. With this in mind I have been soliciting

projects from independent companies and producers for direct to DVD distribution. I came upon a project that had ALL of the features needed to become a major seller. BIG name Hip Hop artists, good filming techniques, strong soundtrack and a built in consumer following for sales.

I approached the company, had them send me a screener and forwarded their information to my clients in California. I also asked the company if they had ALL of the paperwork together to make this deal happen. Clearances on the individuals shot on camera, clearances on the music and ownership (copyright) of the material. Of course the company told me that they had everything I needed especially since I had the money to make this deal happen.

This company was offered a six figure advance, a mid six figure marketing budget and a guarantee for assistance in foreign markets. The contracts were sent and I started waiting for the company to send the required clearances so the check could be cut.

The company did not send in the materials or the contract for over 4 months. Upon further inquiry I finally found out that the person who shot the film never got anyone to sign off on the clearances, had never sent in a copyright form on the movie and had not published or cleared any of the music. ALL OF THIS AFTER THE DEAL HAD BEEN CUT.

Needless to say this project has died a slow death for it can never go to a mass audience. My relationship with the company has deteriorated based on the initial lies that they told and the distributor does not want to work with this company again.

Without the basic preparation this company missed their 15 minutes of fame and thousands of dollars in royalties.
- Allen Johnston

"People don't plan to fail, they FAIL TO PLAN!"

TASKS:

1) **ALWAYS carry a pen.**
2) **Carry a pen and paper to ALL meetings, workshops and conferences.**
3) **Keep business cards and press kits handy.**
4) **Create a folder on your desktop (and laptop) for all your important promotional/ marketing materials. (including bio, discography, history, pictures, ads, reviews, letters…..etc).**
5) **Make sure all legal requirements are met. (copyright, trademark, contracts, releases, permissions…..etc).**

THE SIXTH COMMANDMENT

BUSINESS IS PERSONAL.

CHAPT 6: BUSINESS IS PERSONAL

Don't ever let anyone sell you on the idea that a particular agreement, negotiation or transaction is, "*Business, not personal.*" That's trash! A flat out lie! ALL BUSINESS is conducted off of the springboard of personal relationships.

Imagine this scenario:

It's a Friday night, and you decide to go out to the popular local nightclub owned by your good friend of 10 years. It is an especially chilly night. When you get there, you see your buddy at the entrance of the club. You also notice the line to get in is wrapped around the corner, and the VIP line isn't a much better option. Your friend, the club owner, sees you and motions for you to come to the entrance door. **What is your expectation at this moment?**

Undoubtedly, you are expecting some type of favor from your friend. Maybe he'll let you cut the line. Maybe he'll let you enter without being frisked. Maybe he'll let you in for free. What ever it is, your expectation of special treatment was formed because of your relationship with the club owner. Don't worry, your expectation of favor/ special treatment and the granting thereof is normal everyday practice. It occurs at all levels of any industry; from the *streets*, to the *suites* and even as high as The White House!

Anyone who watched Michael Moore's documentary **Fahrenheit 911** saw how President Bush basically hooked up all his buddies with great jobs in government and international business. It was obvious that many of the people he chose were not the best ones for the positions, but they all benefited from the same "hook-up" system outlined in the nightclub scenario. As long as business continues to be conducted by *persons*, business will forever be **personal**.

LIFE LESSON:

People will give business and lend support to individuals that they like...PERIOD! That's business, and it's personal. As an actress I've had auditions, callbacks, and landed roles because the casting director or production assistant liked me and thought I was "sweet" and "kind". My instinctual response is, "well isn't everyone who is trying to get cast on a movie or television show, sweet, kind, patient, humble, etc". Their answers to me time, and time again are, "No!" There are more "wanna be divas" who play extra roles, are totally unheard of, and are not working actresses, than there are <u>true</u> divas in Hollywood and New York combined!

As a publicist, I am well known and well respected in the entertainment community. However, I am less experienced, I have less training, and fewer "professional" tools at my disposal, than the average publicist in Atlanta. I recently met with a producer from Aftermath records who heard about me through one of his business associates. He said, "Man, I heard that you were quiet like a lamb, but your work is ferocious like a lion". Interesting. Someone that I didn't know came from California to pay me top dollar because of what he heard. After our meeting, he paid for his work upfront, because he said that he felt he could trust me. That's business, and it's always personal.
- Troya Sampson

TASKS:

1) Become a likeable individual.... A *"people"* person.
2) Smile & laugh more.
3) Keep breath mints handy.
4) Be cordial and respectful with strangers. You never know whom an individual knows or may be.
5) Be alert in public. You never know who's watching.
6) Stay in contact with influential people, especially when you DON'T need anything from them. That way, they won't mind you contacting them when you DO need something.
7) Be humble, yet confident.

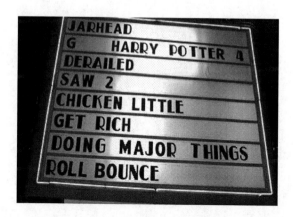

Using the principals of the Hustler's 10 Commandments, Hotep was able to get a movie theater to agree to screen his movie for a week. This is a HUGE accomplishment for any independent filmmaker (not to mention a first-time filmmaker). On opening night, **Independent Doin' Major Things** *ranked #1 at the box office; even beating* **Harry Potter 4***!*

THE SEVENTH COMMANDMENT

EVERYTHING IS NEGOTIABLE, EVERYTHING.

CHAPT 7: EVERYTHING IS NEGOTIABLE, EVERYTHING

Successful people all have very similar characteristics. Most are very bold or brave in some way. They take chances and have confidence. One of the most prominent characteristics I've noted in successful people is an attitude that doesn't permit them to accept things at face value. They simply refuse to accept the cards that are dealt to them.

As a hustler in your field, one of the most powerful beliefs that you can hold is to know that, Everything is negotiable..........EVERYTHING!

Side Note:

Let me clarify and say this. I am not saying that you should think you are *above the law*, go rob a bank and expect not to be arrested. I am simply saying that you need to refuse to settle for anything "*standard*".

"The rule applies to everyone.....except YOU!"

When a lawyer hands you a contract, don't be afraid to negotiate. When a peer says "no", don't take that as the final answer. When a contractor/ company quotes you a price for a service, don't be afraid to talk them down. Remember....... that *contract*, "*no*" and *price quote* was the *standard*, it was not designed for you. It applies to everyone else EXCEPT you; cuz you know that **everything is negotiable**.

LIFE LESSON:

Recently, I needed a rental car for entertaining friends of mine. So before I went to the car rental, I *decided that I was going to ask for the "preferred customer rate". (I thought I made this category up.) As soon as I walked into the car rental office, I looked for the "person in charge." As he approached, he asked if he could help me. I said plainly, "I need your preferred customer weekend rate." "Sure," he responded. I got a **mid size** car for $19.99 per day with unlimited mileage instead of the usual $39.99 per day rate. All it took was me convincing **myself** that I **deserved** the preferred customer rate. The rest was easy. Everything is negotiable. Sign the contract with **yourself** first.*

- Will Coleman, Ph.D.

LIFE LESSON:

Any astute businessperson will tell you that negotiation is an essential part of closing a deal. Even the standard terms found in contracts are negotiable in the art of business. When I did my first movie "The Sun Will Rise", I had to negotiate contracts with crew members and cast. I wanted well-known celebrities to play as my principal characters. Operating on a modest budget, financially, I could not afford their usual rates. However, I knew as social beings, we are all subjective and have changeable opinions.

As a hustler, I was able to negotiate more favorable terms, and the movie was made for less than one-third of the projected cost. If I had not known that everything is negotiable, I would have proved the naysayers right when they stated, "you don't have enough capitol to pull this thing off".

- Rahiem Shabazz

Yes, everything is negotiable......but only if you have the leverage to **negotiate**. What are you bringing to the table? If you haven't established a position of VALUE in the eyes of the opposing side, you may find that you have nothing to negotiate with!

TASKS:

1) **Be confident in yourself AND your offer.**
2) **Find creative ways to BARTER (exchange) services or goods as opposed to paying money for them.**
3) **When negotiating, always remember that the other party is your EQUAL, not superior.**
4) **Make sure that you are negotiating with a person that actually has the *authority* to make the decision. *Never let someone tell you "NO", that can't tell you "YES".***
5) **Have a lawyer look at lengthy contracts before you sign.**
6) **Whenever possible, request or draft contracts in "Lamens" terms instead of *Legalese*. (Legalese is simply the language lawyers use to confuse people that didn't go to law school. It allows them to charge ridiculous prices for their services.)**
7) **Use the term "agreement" instead of *contract*. It is less intimidating to the other party.**
8) **Remember that a contract is simply an agreement between two parties. It can be verbal, written or recorded on tape. It DOES NOT have to be drafted by an attorney to be enforceable. There are even stories of agreements written on <u>napkins</u> that were upheld in a court of law.**

THE EIGHTH COMMANDMENT

IT'S NOT *WHAT* YOU KNOW <u>OR</u> *WHO* YOU KNOW... IT'S WHO KNOWS YOU!

CHAPT 8: IT'S NOT *WHAT* YOU KNOW <u>OR</u> *WHO* YOU KNOW............ IT'S WHO KNOWS YOU

"Life is a game. Losers are those that don't know how to play."

We've already established that much of the game of life is won (or lost) because of relationships. Yes, business is personal, but let me take this idea a step further.

Life is one big popularity contest!

In the entertainment industry there is a popular saying that states, "*It's not **what** you know, it's **who** you know.*" It's with this understanding that people commonly employ a practice known as "*name-dropping*". Name-dropping is when a person makes a point to state that they are acquainted with certain celebrities or influential people. This is done to make the *name-dropper* appear to be important, because he/she knows "important" people. The idea is, to *know* lots of key people in the industry so you can get preferential treatment. (*After all, business IS personal.*)

The fact is: anyone can claim to know somebody else. So, a more important question would be; *Does the celebrity or influential person that you claim to be acquainted with, KNOW YOU?*

It's not *what* you know, or *who* you know..... it's who knows <u>you</u>!

LIFE LESSON:

In my everyday workings, I have tried to network by doing the right thing by others. In turn, my character speaks for itself. Many times over, I may

help someone through my association with different organizations, especially with my alma mater, Morehouse College. As an assistant football coach, I travel throughout the south recruiting. Some students I recruit for football and others just to get a young man in somebody's college or university. I find my self receiving emails, phone calls, letters, and sometimes even office visits from people that have been given my name as a reference point of contact for different opportunities. These opportunities include job offers, student-athletes wanting to transfer to Morehouse College, speaking invitations, amongst others. This is because I put myself in that position to be KNOWN verses trying to know everybody.
- Phillip Thomas

LIFE LESSON:

You can have the best product in the world, but if no one knows it, what's the point? In my city, local radio is very beneficial, especially to the small entertainment companies. However, being that Atlanta's radio market is top 10 in the nation, the cost of a radio advertisement is MAD HIGH! (Like 2 G's for a commercial high.)

My business partner, Abyss, and I had been hustling around the city, hitting every spot on the mic, and passing out our flyers for shows. It just so happened that one of the poets that is a regular on the radio came through our spot and loved the vibe. She in turn invited us to the radio station to meet the personality that put her on every week during her night slot. From that instant, the rest they say is history. We immediately hit it off. This radio personality was sweet, positive, and had genuine love of our art. The poet that invited us through was a good person as well, but still worked a 9 to 5, and wasn't able to get out as often. So we offered the radio personality our street hustle and knowledge of where the hottest of the hot were, in exchange for her knowledge and support of the radio waves. It was, and still is a beautiful marriage. We started producing poetry shows for her, and had instant success. Her listeners really wanted to experience what she did on a weekly basis, but were blown away by the talent that we provided for the events. Again, we knew we had the best product, and people were going to know about it. We were the first company to sell out a 900 seat venue OFF OF POETRY! And we did it a few times. All the while, meeting and building rapports with other radio personalities in different time slots, the promotions team, all the way to the interns. We became part of their family.

- E. Christopher "Cocktails" Cornell

LIFE LESSON:

(This is as real as it gets.) I am an actor out of N.Y. One of the number one questions posed to actor is "Do you have an agent"? I have been in the game for eight years and I have worked with several agents. I like them, I love, and yes to some degree you do need them. I moved to California for a few years, and have been on some of the top T.V. stations and performed in major motion pictures. How? Based off of WHO KNEW ME; that's how. I had established myself in New York and built a rep for myself by working with some good directors, acting coaches, and other fellow actors all who had been in the business longer than myself. I informed these colleagues of my voyage to Hollywood and they did the rest. Some passed

me contact numbers and others even made phone calls on my behalf. The people who knew me, and my ability, got me through doors most people couldn't even imagine. Real Talk. This is an example of what makes this commandment so real for me in my life. Don't get it twisted... an agent is very pertinent and very much necessary, but that is a sad excuse not to get your hustle up, and do what you have to do to get your name known. Peace and God bless.
-Tyson Hall

P.S. Since I have had these experiences, I now refer to God as my agent. Who knows you better than HIM?

TASKS:

1) Revisit tasks for "*Business is Personal*".
2) Develop a good reputation (be honest and pay back debts).
3) Make your physical appearance one that is memorable.
4) When naming your business, use a name that is unique.
5) Create a slogan that is catchy.
6) Turn your corporate identity into one that "stands out".
7) Aggressively promote your business through multiple formats (T.V., radio, flyers, t-shirts, hats, pens.... etc.)

THE NINTH
COMMANDMENT

IT TAKES DOUGH, TO MAKE BREAD.

CHAPT 9: IT TAKES DOUGH, TO MAKE BREAD

Most "business–minded" people understand this one. So, I dedicate this chapter to the *artistic* people.

The day of the "starvin' artist" is dead! There is no nobility and honor in being creative and talented, yet barely able to survive. Survival mode is the lowest level of existence. Roaches "*survive*". As human beings, we should seek to LIVE. In a capitalistic world, in order to live, you need MONEY. Point blank. Get used to it. *Money, money, money, money, money!*

Side Note: The Bible states that the "love" of money is the root of all evil. I'm not saying love money, I'm saying love LIFE!

The vast majority of artists (musical, visual, film, literary) have a nasty habit of foregoing financially beneficial opportunities in pursuit of their "art".

Many quit school, refuse to get a steady job and dress/ alter their appearance in ways that force them to live in marginalized communities filled with other wannabe artists.

The rationale for these actions is often something like, *"I can't continue school or go to work because I'm trying to pursue my artistic career so I can be happy and do my thing."*

The view of school/ work as being an obstacle to artistic goals and happiness is a foolish one indeed. For many, it is just a poor excuse for being **lazy**, **irresponsible** and **broke**.

The mentality of the "starvin' artist" actually undermines the artistic freedom, creativity and integrity that they

69

claim to seek. **Once you make your survival dependent on your art, you place yourself in a position where you often have to compromise your art just to get by (this is known as artistic prostitution, or *selling out*).**

Know this..... EVERYBODY has some type of artistic ability, but many artists fail to recognize the difference between art and BUSINESS!

Business- *a commercial or mercantile activity engaged in as a means of livelihood.*

ARE YOU SEEKING TO TURN YOUR *ART* INTO A **BUSINESS**?

FACT: In the recording business, it is well known that only 10% of the albums released annually make a profit.

This success rate is similar across the board for the movie, fashion and publishing industries.

Few people get paid for their art.
Out of this few, only a **fraction**
make enough money from their art
to SURVIVE.

Instead of selling *art*, many artists end up **"selling-out"** because they finally have to face the fact: when turning art into business, IT TAKES *DOUGH* TO MAKE BREAD.

LIFE LESSON:

When my husband/ producer/ writer passed away in 2002, there was a settlement for wrongful death awarded to me. I took that money and made the

biggest investment of my life....MY WORK!
Though the death of my husband is hard for me
on a daily basis, I knew I must continue our work
and strive for success at all times.

I decided to create a pioneer performance group called
the CAUSTIC DAMES, build a company, recording
studio and executive staff for CAUSTIC
ENTERTAINMENT GROUP, LLC. It was the best
investment I ever made!

Through in-house & internet distribution, in-house
marketing, promotions & manufacturing, I have built
an empire that will sustain many, many, many
generations in my family for years to come,
GENERATIONAL WEALTH!

Now, I run my label and production company and
deposit the checks. It took the settlement money of
my beloved husband's death to really cause a huge
impact for my company's growth financially.

Money is the most important factor when you are
starting a newbusiness. You can't start or run a real
business without it.
- Mimi Johnson

R. I. P. TRUBBLE PHUNK (1964-2002) I love and
miss you dearly.

LIFE LESSON:

I have been in some business or another since I
was 12. Collecting bottles and old newspapers
was my first business. I used to get a penny a
pound for the newspapers and 2 cents per bottle
for the bottles. Back in those days they actually

71

reused the bottles. It didn't take much money to start that business; A wagon and a pair of shoes. My dad spotted me the money for both.

Later on in life, I would become involved in various other money-making ventures. I was the son of a schoolteacher, who worked about 4 jobs to keep food on the table for the six of us. There wasn't too much family "venture capital" money left to fund any of my other ideas so I always had to figure things out on my own.. My 85-year-old mom to this day does not know what I do for a living and often ask why I don't get a real job with the Telephone Company or Gas and Electric Company.

I worked many years as a commissioned salesman. It didn't take much money to get into that business beyond the cost of a few suits and a pair of shoes (my Dad had stopped buying them for me at that point) but it still cost money.

My first business that required more than a pair of shoes to get started was a game business. My buddy and I sold two local grocers on fronting the money needed to get started with that venture. The grocers were given a percentage of the new company.

My current business was started with five credit cards of $5000ea. That business has converted that $25,000 debt into a multi-million dollar publishing services company with thousands of customers.

What does all of the above have to do with you? Unless you just want to go get a job, work forty years and maybe get a pension, it takes money to make money. There are creative ways of coming up with the money but it's up to you. It also may take a couple steps to get to where you want to be. That's no big deal. If what you really want to do costs $10,000 to get started and you only have $1000, you may need to do something that only costs $1000 to get started and save from that until you have $10,000 and then go back to what you wanted to do in the first place.

A word of note: Don't burn bridges. If someone has done you a favor and extended you credit or loaned you money, pay them back.... Always. Not doing so always has a way of coming back to haunt you.

- Ron Pramschufer

TASKS:

1) **Try by all means to finance your ventures with your own money. When you use other people's money you often subject your art / business to their opinions, guidelines and influence. YOU'RE NOT A BUSINESS OWNER IF YOU DON'T _OWN_ YOUR BUSINESS!**
2) **Get a JOB, so you can afford to be a true artist/ visionary...*unbought and unbossed*!**
3) **KEEP A JOB until you can live off of your art/ business alone.**
4) **Get a GOOD financial advisor.**
5) **Seek grants b4 seeking a loan.**

73

6) Look for celebrities, athletes or otherwise extremely rich people to be investors in your vision. These people make great silent partners because they have so much money, and/ or are so busy they don't want to get too involved with your business. (A silent partner is basically someone who provides money to assist with your venture, but doesn't tell you how to run it.)

7) <u>Young people</u>: *STAY IN SCHOOL!* Dropping out of High School in hopes of winning a 1 in 10 gamble is crazy! College will truly be the best years of your life! It is there, that you will build your network of lifetime friends, future Fortune 500 business owners, political leaders and media moguls.

Remember: WEALTH IS NOT AN AMOUNT OF *MONEY*; IT IS A <u>STATE OF MIND</u>. THE WEALTHIEST MAN IS NOT HE WHO HAS THE *MOST*, BUT HE WHO NEEDS THE **LEAST**.

THE TENTH
COMMANDMENT

KNOW & BELIEVE IN THYSELF.

CHAPT 10: KNOW & BELIEVE IN THYSELF

Action, self-reliance, the vision of self and the future have been the only means by which the oppressed have seen and realized the light of their own freedom.
- Marcus Garvey

In order to make the *dough*, *negotiate*, build a great *network*, develop an *image* and deal with being *lonely*; **knowledge of self is key**.

Have you ever seen an individual that appeared to be extremely lucky? Someone who success and happiness seem to follow like a shadow? Imagine reaching a point in your life where **your plans** are directly in line with that which is **planned for you**. This is the power of knowing yourself.

Everyone has a purpose on this earth, a destiny; but few actually realize what their purpose really is. Most people die having spent their entire lives searching to find the reason for their existence. Many work (and will retire from) jobs that they never enjoyed. Those that had the opportunity to try different careers, usually give up the search to *"find their place in the world"* after experiencing too many failed attempts. *To live a purpose driven life is a blessing indeed!*

From birth, each of us has been bestowed with divine gifts. We call these gifts *talents*. Comic books call these gifts...... **powers**. I like to think that we each have 3 missions in life. 1) to find out what our gifts are, 2) to hone our skills, and 3) use our talents for the betterment of the world.

The first is the most difficult of the 3 missions. How does one get to know his self? I think *experience* is the best teacher. God uses our life experiences to speak to us. Unfortunately, most people fail to see the **lessons** in their experiences; particularly, the "*bad*" ones.

Everything happens for a reason.

When people say this statement they often forget that it applies to the bad things as well as the good things. When life "happens", take time to analyze the role you played in making the situation occur; also reflect on how your response made the situation *better* or *worse*. This will teach you a lot about yourself. It should also empower you to realize how much your own actions affect your life experiences (good OR bad).

The saddest thing in this world is wasted talent.

Recognize your natural talents; the things that come easiest to you. School is a great place to start. What were the things you were good at in school? Were you a great writer, mathematician, artist, speaker, athlete? **View school as an opportunity to hone your talents!** College is the stone on which you sharpen your sword for the battle called life!

Use what you *got*, to get what you want.

Many people are overwhelmed by the battle of life. They suffer continuous losses because they pursue goals that are not in-line with their natural blessings. **It is almost sinful for you to NOT utilize the gifts God has bestowed you with**. Maybe life wouldn't be so hard if people stopped *searching* for blessings, and started *using* the ones they have already received.

All of your gifts, talents and natural skills can lead to a career or business that you enjoy and feel a sense of purpose when performing. Best of all, your life will be relatively *"easy"* because you built your welfare off of things that come naturally.

The difference between heroes and villains is the carrying out of Good, or Evil acts.

Just like Super-heroes, we can use our talents for the betterment or detriment of the world. The following is an excerpt from an article I wrote for a magazine. I think it appropriately shows the power of self-knowledge.

Knowledge Of Self was a popular phrase in Hip-Hop culture during the late eighties and early nineties. It's no surprise that this era is commonly referred to as "The Golden Age" of Hip-Hop. We were shining! Not just from the rope chains, but from knowing that we are descendents of Kings and Queens, Gods and Earths.

In the mid-nineties, the "criminal culture" was allowed to invade Hip-Hop. Kings and Queens were reduced to Thugs, Pimps and Hoes. Drug use and selling became "cool". Criminals became heroes. The "G" in Kool G Rap went from standing for Genius, to meaning Gangsta. (Damn....that's deep!)

Understand This: PEOPLE ACT IN ACCORDANCE TO HOW THEY VIEW THEMSELVES.

Today's Hip-Hop (black urban) culture lacks true knowledge of self. This void has been replaced with an IMAGE of Gangstas, Thugs, Pimps and Hoes.

So, when we "get our hustle on", instead of identifying with our royal-selves to make earth changing power moves, many of us mis-use our abilities for common street hustles that have us constantly on the run from po-po. This is what is known as "The Trap."

The life of one of the world's greatest hustlers, Malcom X, is the perfect example of how Knowledge Of Self can transform ones life. Peep how his hustle abilities went from "street corner" to "earth mover" once he learned who he truly was.

If you really want to step your game up, instead of wasting money on weed, and alcohol.........buy a book. Instead of the strip club, visit a museum. Watch the history channel, instead of Scarface (for the 30th time). Instead of freestyle ciphers, participate in a knowledge-building cipher. Real hustlers and gangstas make matter move, BUT also make moves that matter. Ask Carter "G" Woodson. (AUC Magazine Feb 2006)

Believing in yourself is easy. Once you have gained knowledge of self you will have also realized that God has been with you every step of your life's journey. In fact, you would have learned that God was not only **with** you, he was **WITH-IN** you as well. What better reason to believe in yourself is there?

TASKS:

1) **Take a personality test.**
2) **Meditate.**
3) **Recognize that God is *within you*, as much as he is all around you.**

4) Study your history/ culture.
5) Video tape yourself so you can see yourself the way others see you.
6) Study human psychology.
7) Self- analyze.
8) Go to a college outside of your hometown.
9) Ask people their opinion of you.
10) Ask people their first impression of you.
11) Read other self-empowerment books.
12) Identify & *Utilize* your strengths.
13) Identify & *Improve* on your weaknesses.
12) Read this book again!

THE FINAL ANALYSIS

The moral of the story is: *Life is what YOU make it!*

YOU are in control!
YOU are responsible!
YOU are at fault!
YOU can change it!

If you can imagine life being a popular video game; YOU are the one that holds the controller. The more you *"play"*, the better your skills get. You learn how to navigate more easily. Your use of time becomes more efficient. If you *"lose"*, you hit the **continue** button and press on. You keep going because that is the ONLY way you can eventually **win**.

Following this analogy, I hope you use **The Hustler's 10 Commandments** like a manual for this intense video game called *Life*. It is a reference guide that provides easy answers to difficult questions. Refer to it as often as necessary for *"insider tips"*. Not to be confused for short-cuts, the principals herein give you a better understanding of the dynamics of the game, which in turn, will ultimately make you a better *player*.

Peace & Power!

- Hotep

A NOTE TO THE LADIES:

Ladies,

Please know that you are the most powerful being on this planet. I know what I'm going to say in the next few paragraphs will seem strange to you at first. But, I promise, after I'm done, it will all begin to make sense.

"You can tell the strength of a nation, by noting the condition of its women."

The Point:

Women run the world. This fact is the very reason why they are oppressed so heavily. Women are more powerful than they know. You see, man will do ANYTHING to be embraced by a beautiful woman's love, care and sexuality. 90% of men's actions are done for the sake of women.

A woman is the only force on earth that can drive the sane man CRAZY, turn the intelligent man FOOLISH, and make the disciplined man lose CONTROL. This is a very unsettling fact for man to live with. As logical beings, man cannot live with the possibility of being rendered to an emotional SLOB because of a woman.

In order to protect his fragile ego, man devised ways to control woman.

The idea was to make woman feel inferior so she can be kept in her place and not hurt man. Traditionally, man used physical strength, money and education (or lack thereof) to subdue woman and keep her in a position of severe dependence. Over time, man developed other methods of "*control*" such as by employing **sexism**, **racism** and even using **religion**.

Let's keep it real!

All the great, life-giving forces known to us are given female attributes: mommy, Mother Earth, Mother Nature. How then, did GOD, the most powerful, omniscient life giver of all, become known as the "*Heavenly Father*"?

On a microbiological level, the X chromosome (which the female) is stronger than the Y (male) chromosome. In the great race to fertilize a woman's egg, the Y sperm are weaker and die quicker. (That is why more women are born to the earth than men). Also, if you look at the X and Y chromosomes under a microscope, you will note that the Y is nothing more than an X that is missing a "leg".

Any man of greatness (including myself) will admit that he was able to attain his wealth and power ONLY BECAUSE OF THE WOMAN (or women) that stands beside, behind and sometimes beneath him.

So woman, while you're out getting your hustle on in this "man's world", remember your true place in it. IF MAN IS KING, THEN YOU ARE QUEEN, *THE MOST POWERFUL PIECE IN A CHESS GAME*.

- Hotep

A NOTE TO PARENTS & EDUCATORS:

Over the course of my 10-year teaching career, I've noticed that our public educational system fails our youth miserably. Not because it is inferior, but because of how we teach our youth to use it. We basically tell children that they should **get an education, so they can be smart, so they can pursue a degree, that will land them a good job, and make them a lot of money, so they can be happy.**

Well, besides wrongfully equating money with happiness, we as a society also make the mistake of **lying** to our youth.

We live in a country where high school dropouts become millionaires, and college graduates struggle living check to check. In our great nation, a person can make more money throwing a ball, than ones who save lives, educate our future and protect our civil liberties..... **combined!**

The high school dropout rate in some areas is up to **50%** because our youth know the old model of *"go to school to get a good job"* is dead. **Why should they bother going to school?**

The TRUTH shall set you free!

The *Hustler's 10 Commandments* are based off of true, real-life success stories, best practices, common sense, and ancient wisdom. The practice of these ideals compels the reader to seek greatness; ALL READERS, yes, **even our hardheaded youth!**

Instead of viewing school as an *obstacle*, they will begin to see it as an **opportunity!** They will see their teachers as **allies**, as opposed to *enemies*. They will understand that **it's lonely at the top**, and therefore, won't be afraid to excel when most fail. Peer pressure will be less of a problem. They will know that their **network is their net worth**, so they will choose their friends more wisely. They will want to dress more appropriately, because they learned that **image is everything**. They will show up to class early because they understand how **the early bird gets the worm**. They will take a renewed interest in history and science, so they can **know their self**. They will actually seek to improve their writing, reading and speaking skills because they now see the TRUE connection between school, the real world and their own lives as future leaders, inventors, educators, entrepreneurs and, (as I like to put it)... *hustlers*!

*"The **ULTIMATE HUSTLER** is one who is both book smart and street smart. He/she is able to take their good education, combine it with common sense, to make dollars and cents!"*

–Hotep, CEO Skinnymen Productions

BREAKDANCE
Copyright 2003

The strobe light's in full effect tonight,
my gold rope's glistening……. it reflect the light.
Expect the wife to be upset,
it's only right that a brother go out and do his thing no
regrets.
The local radio station's havin' Old School Night,
I'm almost 30,
and fit the category.
My life's now surrounded by move- fakers,
it felt good to see brothers when they broke out the
windbreakers.
I was the type,
on the opposite side,
scoping the hype,
got a brother open tonight,
like sitting front row at an Ali fight,
or the first time you ever heard Rapper's Delight.
We was just teens,
Mantronix hit the scene,
honey dips in their Bengal earrings,
always caught my eye,
under fresh Cazelles,
that I boosted from 42nd and Canal.

I represent grown folks and showboats,
bicycles, we put the cards in our own spokes.
I take a fat black marker and write love,
for anyone who ever wore a shiny white glove,
and spun, on linoleum,
the Royal Crown Petroleum,
to make waves…..
stocking caps with a hole in them.
No doubt,
it was better than armor,
in the 6th Grade with a new black leather bomber.

In fact, I always wanted a sheepskin,
but moms was cheap then,
I never got more than a hat.
Striped Lee's and shell toes,
musta' been the fact that hell froze,
who ever thought the sh*t would come back.

In '89 hot shot in Nintendo,
used to have crazy dreams: fancy cars and limos.
Hip-Hop creshendo,
write with a broken pencil,
now they all call me Mr. Benzo.
Doin' a show up in SoHo,
bums on the street tryin' ta get my dough….
I said "No".
Used to rock beats on promos,
now we shake hands with the lames and momos.
I know it's sick.
Stop dis-ease,
brother's used to rock for free,
now we play Monopoly.
And we cop with ease,
all properties,
and material items for girls that's knock knee'd.
I go for broke.
Look at the state of the world,
I show them hope,
travel upstream……. in a rowboat.
Player, I got more bars than soap.
Forever holding it down,
my vision is long scope.

-Hotep, CEO Skinnymen Productions

ABOUT THE AUTHOR:

Hotep is owner and operator of **Skinnymen Productions;** an independent multimedia EDU-tainment company based in Atlanta, GA. Since 1997, Hotep has been a pioneer in Atlanta's entertainment/ media industries. Hotep is the producer, writer and director of the landmark documentary, *Independent, Doin' Major Things*, founder of the quarterly newspaper, *The Progress Report* and creator of the exotic art series, **The Venus Revolution**.

If being recognized as a gifted artist, speaker and visionary weren't enough, Hotep (a Morehouse college grad), is also a ten year veteran educator in the Dekalb County School System in Georgia.

Skinnymen Productions is dedicated to creating projects that are equally **entertaining**, as they are **educational** and **empowering**. They provide the bridge between *technology, scholarship, history, popular urban culture and social issues*. As a speaker, Hotep encourages media control and artistic independence by teaching self-empowerment, practical strategies, financial tips, best practices and wisdom gained through over 15 years of experience in the entertainment industry.

BOOK HOTEP AS A GUEST SPEAKER AT YOUR NEXT EVENT OR CONFERENCE!

404-294-7165

WWW.SKINNYMEN.COM

CONTRIBUTING WRITERS:

 Nancy Gilliam is an accomplished performing artist, author and teacher. Her media credits include working with the MGM and ABC Television.Her author credits include: the companion study guide to the biography for Lebron James, "Chicken Soup for the African American Soul" and "Chicken Soup for the African American Woman's Soul".A true believer in empowerment and education, she is the co-founder of the African American Literary & Media Group.

 Will Coleman, Ph.D. is Co-Founder and Co-Director of the Black Kabbalah Institute. It is a nonsectarian organization that is designed to teach and apply principles of the Hebrew mysticism for the enrichment of African/Americas spiritual and psychological health. He is an ordained minister and Theologian-in-Residence at First Afrikan Church in Lithonia, Georgia.

 Allen Johnston created THE MUSIC SPECIALIST website (www.asha.com); a website dedicated to education of the entertainment industry. His latest book "Publishing Quick & Easy" is a mainstay for new and experienced attorneys. Currently, Mr. Johnston develops International & National movie, audio and publishing deals for major and independent artists and film makers.

 Queen is an internationally known spoken word artist from South Jersey. Queen has appeared on many national television networks, such as, BET's 106 and Park, NBC, UPN and the likes. With two published books, and two albums, she is now writing and producing movies. Queen has toured the US several times. To find out more about Queen, visit www.Justqueen.net.

Mr. Shabazz is a recognized hip-hop journalist with credentials in writing video treatments, movie scripts, bios, press releases, magazine articles, and online articles. As owner of RASHA ENTERTAINMENT LLC, Rahiem produced the feature film, "The Sun Will Rise". He is in the process of negotiating for the picture's worldwide distribution. Currently, he is working on his first novel titled "Love On Lay-Away".

Omar Tyree, a New York Times best-selling author and 2001 NAACP Image Award recipient for Outstanding Literature in Fiction, has sold more than 1.4 million copies of books worldwide. Most recently, Tyree began Flyy Girl Incorporated, based on his most successful novel and beautiful career women of color. He also plans to launch a book-related television program to reinforce the seriousness of African-American literature. For more on Omar Tyree, goto (*www.OmarTyree.com*)

Tyson is a native New Yorker; his roots run deep into the pulse of the NY cultural/theater scene. His love for fashion/music/dance drew him to the stage as a model and dancer. After Graduating John Jay College, Tyson threw himself into developing his newly found talents in Drama. His professionalism has elevated his worth and given him work with respected directors and films, such as, **"PAID IN FULL"** and television roles on **New York Undercover**, **Moesha** and **OZ**.

Ron Pramschufer is one of the founders of RJ Communications and Booksjustbooks.com. He co-invented and marketed two highly successful satirical political board games. The idea of RJ Communications and Booksjustbooks.com evolved from a combination of past experiences in the production office of a book manufacturer, in a pressroom bindery-shipping department and as a partner in a small press publisher. *Contact Ron at ron@rjcom.com*.

Phillip Thomas is an assistant football coach at his alma mater, Morehouse College. He is active in community service ventures through non-profit organizations where he sits as a board member of 99ways Youth Foundation and The Project Friendship Foundation. Phil is also completing course work for obtaining his doctorate degree in Educational Leadership. Phil resides in Ellenwood, Georgia.

Troya Sampson is an actress, publicist and former educator. She has landed roles in feature films such as *The Gospel*, *Madea's Family Reunion*, and *ATL*, as well as other independent films and shorts. In addition to pursuing acting, Troya is working independently as a publicist for various artists in the entertainment industry. One of Troya's favorite quotes of is, "success is a journey, not a destination".

Mimi Johnson has operated Caustic Entertainment Group, LLC, since the death of her husband in 2002 alone. She is responsible for all of the bookings, executive production, copyrights/ publishing of their work, manufacturing and distribution of their product which includes current CD, "ESTROGEN LOVE LP". Go to www.causticdames.com for more info.

Tarik Scott aka Big Tah, CEO of BTM, National Director of Dynamic Producer, Co CEO of World Premiere and Co Manager of Willie Joe. Big Tah has a BA in Music Industry Studies/Marketing. He is a self-professed Marketing Genius and applies it to many hats such as event planning, artist management, consultation and promotions.

94

E. Christopher "Cocktails" Cornell is author of Cocktails Commentary: Volume 1 and the founder of Live Poets Society, L.L.C with his business partner, HBO Def Poet, Derrick "Abyss" Graham. Along with producing quality spoken word events, the company offers a multi-faceted approach to events planning. Cocktails has appeared on MTV Road Rules 11 and is one of the feature entertainers on Joyce Littel's Love and Relationship Cruise for V-103. Visit **www.livepoets.net** for more info.

Keisha Perry is an Entertainment Attorney licensed to practice in Georgia. Ms. Perry worked as a Business Law Consultant for Better Communications, Inc. where she was primarily responsible for entity formations for small business owners. Since establishing The Perry Law Group, Ms. Perry has led entity formations for independent labels, drafted and negotiated contracts for artists, producers, and songwriters. Ms. Perry has the tenacity, knowledge, and perseverance that it takes to be successful and build long-term and prosperous working relationships.

PRAISE FOR THE HUSTLER'S 10 COMMANDMENTS:

Below are excerpts from a few of the hundreds of letters and emails I've received in response to **The Hustler's 10 Commandments**. It is truly an honor to have created something that has touched so many people, from such varied backgrounds in a positive way.

What's good Hotep,

First of all, I just wanted to say that The Hustler's 10 Commandments is definitely the young entrepreneur's guide to getting started and maintaining success in business, whether it be music or whatever. I've been reading it alongside the 48 Laws of Power by Robert Greene and I feel like I have enough knowledge now to make me a successful businessman. Thank you for the jewel my brother. I look forward to purchasing more of your materials in the near future.

Laurence "L. Real" D.

Hotep, You don't know me but my name is Shawn Richards and I just finished reading your book. What's funny is that it didn't actually hit me that I was actually reading a 'Personal development' type book until I got to the very end and you gave the analogy of the video game. But anyway, I just felt compelled to send u a quick note to let u know that I really loved the book. I hope u sell mad copies, it's something that EVERYONE should read. And I wish you continued success in all your dealings in the future.

Shawn

Hotep, I recently bought 3 copies of your book. I was walking throughout the mall and I walked past the shop where your display was at. I saw you and the book and kept on walking. While I was walking away something stood out to me. I guess it was the title. So I turned around and decided to come back and try out your book. I got a copy and I also got a flyer from you with the hustler's 10 commandments on it. As I walked away I read the flyer and I could tell right then that your book was something that would be inspirational to me and some of my friends so I turned around and got 2 more copies and went about my way. I just finished reading your book and I must say that I am very, very impressed and it has also given me some more inspiration. Thank you.

Sincerely,

Steven H.

Hey Hotep, how's it going? My name is Max. I am the Personal Trainer that you met a month ago. I remember we spoke for about 5 minutes. The Hustler's Ten Commandments really hit home with me. Being a Fitness Coach/Personal Trainer I feel like I practice a lot of your commandments. I read it every day so that I can get my mind right and get prepared for another day of hustling. I also sent it to some of my friends so that they can be inspired by your words. Thank you again.

Max

Hotep,

What's up, bro. I am writing in regards to your book The Hustler's Ten Commandments. My mom attended the Black Expo in Jacksonville Fl. and she bought your book. When I saw her later she gave it to me and I finished it an hour later. Let me just say I thought it was great!

I was tempted to email you right away, but I decided that I'd wait a bit to gather my thoughts. As a writer and filmmaker I found the book very intriguing. When I was a kid I was fascinated with the Art of War by Sun Tzu, and I read many translations and commentaries. But I never encountered one that had black commentary. In fact, before I read your book that thought never even occurred to me.

Erle R. G.

Hotep, I wanted to share another testimonial with you. There was a kid, about 17 years old, sitting in the audience at the Book Expo. He stood up and asked the panel *"How do I get my spoken-word out there? Like published? I don't know what to do."* I didn't find that anyone on there gave him any solid advice, so I slid him a note that said, *"Don't leave without talking to me!"* He came to my booth, where his mother picked up a copy of your book for him (he has the audio CD too). Here's the email that he sent me today:

Hey Neece:

I finally got it done (my myspace). I'm not finished hooking it up though. Also, yesterday I finished

HOTEP's Book. WOOOOOOO, it's FIRE. To me it's like The Science of Getting Rich (by Wallace Wattles) specifically for black people. I would love to help getting 10,000 of those books out.

Peace and Blessings
Josh E.

I highly recommend this book to every person who dares to dream. It speaks to the heart of who we are and is a true roadmap of survival for our generation. The commandments are priceless and will motivate our youth to strive for excellence in every area of their lives. We are pleased that Hotep has chosen to share this jewel with our young people.

Coretta C.
Residential Coordinator
Covenant House Georgia

Dear Hotep,

Thanks for the books I received for my students. I passed them out 2 days before the last day of the school year as a graduation gift. Most of my students began reading it immediately after I passed them out and even though I had a lesson scheduled for that day, I cancelled it to let them get into their reading. The last thing I want to do is stop 8th graders from actually getting into a book on their own for once!

I received nothing but great feedback from students who had either finished the book by the end of that day or the following day. They all wanted to know if there was a second part coming out.

I've decided to use the book next school year as a teaching tool. I will have the students read it during second semester and we'll discuss one chapter a day for 2 weeks. I also hope to have you visit our class and talk with students directly.

Again, thanks for your generous gift and I look forward to sharing "The Hustler's 10 Commandments" with my incoming students.

Sincerely,

Sebastien Elkouby
8th Grade Teacher
Global Awareness through Hip Hop Program
The Accelerated School

ETERNAL THANKS,

Hotep

HUSTLE WHILE YOU WORK

· The difference between a job and YOUR BUSINESS.

· The benefits of keeping your day job.

· How to manage your boss.

· How to better manage your time.

· How to make money while you sleep.

· How to find your own, unique commodity.

· How to create Multiple Streams of Income.

· How to finance your business without creating debt.

· The top jobs to have, while getting your hustle on.

· When/ how to quit your job.

· Everything you need to know before starting your business.

The Hustler's Guide
To The
Entertainment Industry

Limited Edition

R.A.B. PRESENTS A SKINNYMEN PRODUCTIONS FILM
"The Hustler's Guide To The Entertainment Industry"
CO-PRODUCED BY ERAJ MEDIA   MUSIC BY SKINNYMEN PRODUCTIONS
WRITTEN AND DIRECTED BY HOTEP   EDITED BY SKINNYMEN PRODUCTIONS

WARNING:

IF YOU CAN'T HANDLE THE TRUTH,

THIS FILM IS <u>NOT</u> FOR YOU!

THE HUSTLER'S GUIDE TO THE ENTERTAINMENT INDUSTRY is for a special breed of entrepreneur. The DVD features the award-winning documentary, **Independent Doin' Major Things (IDMT)**. Using Atlanta, GA as the backdrop, IDMT openly exposes longstanding trade secrets and unethical practices in the entertainment industry. NEVER BEFORE have celebrities and top-level industry executives gone on camera to give such riveting testimonies. Critics and fans alike have nicknamed IDMT, *"The Entertainment Industry's Fahrenheit 911"*. Now jam-packed with new footage, a new name and look, this special-edition re-release is more potent than ever!

THE HUSTLER'S GUIDE TO THE ENTERTAINMENT INDUSTRY dispels many myths and lies that are commonly upheld by the media. Then, it lays the blueprint for how indie **artists, filmmakers, authors** and **entrepreneurs** are able to compete with the majors. After watching, you'll never pay big money for another conference, festival or performance opportunity again!

Extra DVD Features: Theatrical Debut, U.S. Tour Footage, Music Videos and Making the Video, Venus Revolution Art Show (You gotta see this to believe it!)

AVAILABLE ON CD: